VICTORIAN MUSIC COVERS

EAM

VICTORIAN Music Covers

by Doreen and Sidney Spellman

with a Foreword by Sacheverell Sitwell

NOYES PRESS

Noyes Building
Park Ridge, New Jersey, 07656

238675

First U.S. Edition: 1972
Copyright © 1969 by Doreen and Sidney Spellman
Library of Congress Catalogue Card Number: 72-76733
ISBN: 0-8155-5004-9
Printed in Great Britain

List of Illustrations

Foreword

Only a glance through the illustrations to this book on Victorian Music Covers must remind me inevitably of the comedians and 'eccentrics' I have watched 'upon the boards'; Marie Lloyd, whom it is true I never saw at her best; Ella Shields as 'Burlington Bertie'; Vesta Tilley; Nellie Wallace (as perfect a comic dancer as Groucho Marx, with parrot-mask, taking her curtain, fingering the lime feathers in her hat to a few steps of the Charleston); George Robey, in his bowler hat and unfrocked clergyman's guise; Little Tich, again a marvellous comic dancer, whom the immortal Nijinski asked to be taken to see when in London in his brief season before the 1914 war, and whom he admired as a master of 'make up'; the staccato 'machine-gun' delivery of T.E. Dunville; and how many more! And not a microphone between the lot of them. They could be heard without that in every seat in the largest theatre. I recall walking past the Coliseum on a summer afternoon and pausing on the pavement for a moment by the open doors to listen to Vesta Tilley, whom I could see in my mind's eye in her characteristic stride up and down before the footlights.

Now the marvel of these music covers is how they recapture for us the mid-Victorian scene. And Alfred Concanen is on all accounts the most remarkable of the artists concerned. An Irishman from Co. Galway, he must have arrived in London in the 1860s and taken at once to the music-hall and theatre. His output of lithographic music covers may have run to many hundreds, if not thousands. As they are still catalogued in the British Museum Library, I believe, under the song composer's name, and not the artist's, it is near to impossible to arrive at any definitive opinion of his work. A convivial character, no doubt, and no stranger to the theatre bar during the interval, his best when really assured or interested is superb, and though so different in approach, would have had appeal, we may be certain, to Toulouse-Lautrec. The speculative Concanen covers are not so far behind the woodcut prints of Japanese actors; his lithograph differing very much in 'state', as would be seen, I think, in the finest Concanen cover known to me, which is *The Age of*

6

Paper. I wish it were reproduced here, but how many hundreds there are to choose from!

We see this minor artist of high talents in two covers for operettas by Lecocq. Concanen reproduces the actual scene in *Les Pres St Gervais;* while the conspiratorial scene from *Madame Angot* derives additional interest from its music being arranged by Charles Louis Napoleon d'Albert, no less. And was he, or was he not, parent to Eugene d'Albert, opera composer and pianist, next only in some opinions to Liszt, born improbably in Glasgow in 1864? Were I near a musical dictionary and not, as I write this, snowbound in the deep country, I would know the answer. Such are crowded scenes by Concanen, but, also, he is master of the single figure print for music-hall artist or 'eccentric'. His range and variety are remarkable, down to the amusing 'Too Utterly, Utter' aesthete-with-sunflower cover which must date from the 1880s.

And then it all comes to an end. There are no more song covers. But what a wealth of covers and draughtsmen there is to choose from! What a delight to have dear old George Cruikshank in his wonderful little scenes or vignettes from *Fairy Songs and Ballads for the Young!* Second only to Concanen comes John Brandard who is altogether in another vein. He died young in 1863, but as his subjects were drawn from opera and ballet and appealed to a richer public than the music-hall, he had the advantage of more expensive printing and lithography than Concanen. He is lacking in the latter's pungency and wit, but drew the dancers of the Romantic Ballet to perfection, studied their attitudes, and made a speciality for accurate portraiture and of their feet and hands. There were lesser men as well, but these two are the unrivalled portrayers of the Victorian theatre and the London street scene. They, and the spangled Hoxton prints, are the popular arts of Cockney London.

January 1969

On 10 November 1886 Alfred Concanen died. His death marked the end of an era in which he had been a dominating figure. He was one of the select company of lithographers of Victorian music covers, whose work has only come to be appreciated in recent years.

The best of these covers compare favourably with the work of famous artists of the time. They also portray a true picture of life in Victorian London and elsewhere. The worst of them were dominated by crudeness and sentimentality. The craftsmanship was wonderful but discrimination and taste were almost non-existent.

Alfred Concanen was born in 1835 and married twice. His first wife was one of two sisters who were known as the 'Devonshire Beauties' and his second wife was Sarah Cohen. Terence de Marney, the actor, and Derrick de Marney, the actor and film producer, who calls his company 'Concanen Films', are the grandchildren of Sarah and Alfred. Obviously the tradition of entertainment still lives with the family.

Concanen was the chronicler of the 'lion comique'—the music-hall artistes who portrayed the swells and dandies of the mid-Victorian era—and of the music-hall. Performers who would have been forgotten years ago have been immortalized by Concanen. He often portrayed artistes dressed in the costumes in which they appeared for famous songs. On this cover the action has been captured as though by a camera, but with more impact.

H. J. Byron, who wrote *The Continong,* produced nearly 150 plays and burlesques. He was very popular and acted in many of his own plays. His production of *Our Boys* at the Criterion Theatre (where he was manager), ran for over 1,300 performances—a record at that time.

W. Meyer Lutz, the composer of the music, was a conductor of various orchestras in the big London theatres.

The characters portrayed are Mephistopheles, Faust and Marguerite. H. J. Byron's approach to Goethe's theme of Faust clearly was less than reverent.

The Continong : *Alfred Concanen*

8

NIGHTLY ENCORED.

THE CONTINONG.

W. Meyer Lutz, Gaiety Theatre Stra

permission to Sing this Song in Public, apply to

Alfred Concanen Lith

SUNG BY

MISS FARREN, MISS VAUGHAN & MR TERRY,

IN

H. J. BYRON'S BURLESQUE OF LITTLE DOCTOR FAUST,

WORDS BY

HENRY J. BYRON,

MUSIC BY

W. M. LUTZ.

ELGAR BROS.
MUSIC CELLER
WORCESTER,

ENT. STA. HALL   LONDON, CRAMER & C^O 201, REGENT STREET, W

Price 4/=

Whatever the subject, Concanen injected vitality into his illustrations. His treatment of the *Soldaten Leben Waltz* brings the days of cavalry right back to life. The badge shows these were the 17th Lancers. The mention of Herrn Major Von Vittinghoff was probably explained by the fact that many Hanoverians were officers in the British Army, and these Germans actually introduced the lance to England.

The Lancer's hat was called a *Tschapka,* a Polish word. The Poles had reintroduced lances to Europe after a long absence and all Lancers, of whatever nationality, wore hats of this sort.

This cover dates from 1878 and is a late example of Concanen's work. The spotlighting of the figure in the foreground with all its detail contrasts with the blurred supporting figures behind. The flying flags emphasize the movement in the picture and the glamour of the cavalry.

It is possible that the Herrn Major was one of Concanen's immaculate heavy beaux in civilian life, those toffs who dressed in the height of fashion and who were to be seen in Belgravia and in theatre-land. They disappeared with their world in 1914, never to return.

Soldaten Leben Waltz: *Alfred Concanen*

10

SOLDATEN LEBEN

WALTZ.

DEDICATED TO HERRN MAJOR VON VITTINGHOFF.

BY

ALBERT HARTMANN.

MUS. DOC. M. B. OXON.

LONDON, J. B. CRAMER & C.O 201, REGENT S.T W.

ALSO BY THE SAME COMPOSER CLEOPATRA'S NEEDLE WALTZ 4/

ENT. STA HALL

Pr. 4/

Concanen produced book illustrations as well as numerous music covers. His work was confined to lithography but his range of subjects was far wider. Among the best of his portraits were those of The Great Vance and George Leybourne, who might have been forgotten had they not been depicted by Concanen.

Those two artists were the first and most famous of the 'lion comiques'. George Leybourne was born in 1842 and died in 1884. His best-known song was *Champagne Charlie* and from the day it was first performed he became known by that name. He was born Joe Saunders, and came to London from the Midlands as an obscure performer. He modelled his stage character on the toffs of the West End, with their toppers, striped pants and whiskers. His success was tremendous and in a short time he was earning £120 a week, an astronomical sum in those days.

Concanen portrayed Leybourne and The Great Vance in the characters of their songs time and time again. Although they differed in style they were in constant competition. When Leybourne had all London singing *Champagne Charlie*, Vance retaliated with *Cliquot*. In time they made their way through most of the wine-cellar. Many of the songs of the period related to the theme of drink. Concanen's full-length figures are, unlike much fussy Victorian art, tasteful and simple.

With Leybourne and Vance glamour entered into the music-hall. Leybourne's public image was built up by the use of extravagant show business gimmicks. He drove to various London music-halls in which he was appearing in a carriage drawn by four white horses, given to him by Holland, his impressario. His handsome looks, fine voice and stage presence made him the most popular stage performer of the day.

Leybourne's picture on the front of sheet music would certainly have increased sales. The idolatry which today's 'pop' artistes inspire is no new phenomenon. The Victorians had a highly developed live entertainment industry—there were over 500 music-halls in the London area alone—and the music covers were an essential part of it.

I'm on the Teetotal: *Alfred Concanen*

I'M ON THE TEETOTAL.

WRITTEN BY

F. C. BURNAND ESQRE.

SUNG WITH THE GREATEST SUCCESS

BY

GEORGE LEYBOURNE.

Price 3/-

LONDON;
HOPWOOD & CREW, 42, NEW BOND ST. W.

STANNARD & SON, LITHO T

Concanen's family originally came from Galway. One of his ancestors was an artist in the area in the 1760s. Concanen was the archetypal Irishman: colourful, sociable and fiery-tempered. His association with his partner Thomas Lee ended suddenly, possibly after a violent quarrel. Many years after he died his daughter, while going through her father's possessions, insisted on destroying everything associated with Lee. These included covers which they had jointly produced and signed.

La Fille de Madame Angot was one of the many covers Concanen made with Lee. Thomas Lee (1833-1910) originally had been apprenticed to Packer, as so many other good artists were, and in 1856 he met Robert Mallyon. For some years Concanen, Mallyon and Lee worked together. Often a cover might be produced either by two or the three of them, possibly with the aid of an apprentice. A cover signed 'Concanen and Lee' would probably indicate Concanen had done the drawing and Lee the processing. When 'del lith.' appears on a cover it is fair to assume that the delineator also was the lithographer and did the job from start to finish.

Madame Angot came from the Charles Louis Napoleon d'Albert factory which mass-produced all sorts of music for dancing and home consumption.

D'Albert was born near Hamburg in 1809 and emigrated to England with his family in 1816. He became the ballet master at Covent Garden and the King's Theatre. He eventually devoted himself to teaching and composing. The British Museum Library lists hundreds of D'Albert's works, many of which were adapted from popular operatic and dance numbers by other composers.

La Fille de Madame Angot was composed by the Frenchman Lecocq, and was first produced in Brussels in 1872 where it ran for 500 nights.

Concanen's treatment of this theme is exciting and rich, and shows a strong affinity with French style. This stage scene is caricatured almost in the manner of Daumier and does not seem out-dated even 100 years later.

La Fille de Madame Angot: *Alfred Concanen*

LANCERS.

BY

CHARLES D'ALBERT

Int. Sta. Hall.

CHAPPELL & Cº   BOOSEY & Cº
50, New Bond Sᵗ   28, Holles Sᵗ

The business of entertainment was in the Concanen family. Both his father and son were in the trade. While his best work is superb, much of it is mediocre. His world was London and the citizens of London. Even if he were illustrating a seaside scene the people would always be dressed in the height of fashion. He was himself typical of his subjects. He made and spent money quickly and lived a full and colourful life, happiest in the company of theatrical people, writers and intellectuals and in the twilight world of the music-halls. He was a noted raconteur and immensely popular.

Walking through the streets of London, giving pennies to poor children and quickly sketching them at play was one of Concanen's main pleasures. He drew one cover which shows his daughter on the back of an elephant in a parade. He had a prodigious memory for detail and sometimes recalled long-ago scenes for use in his illustrations. However, he was inclined to sacrifice detail and reality for atmosphere.

That's the way to the Zoo is characteristic of the best of Concanen's contemporary scene covers. In these compositions he has bequeathed a detailed record of the costumes, gestures and expressions of a world that has died. Passing fashions, outmoded forms of transport and working-class types who no longer exist are all shown in this picture. We often look back to times like these we think we can remember, but what we actually recall are the tales and scenes of our grandparents' childhood.

Albany Street still has many of its original Nash features. Regent's Park remains as it was but the people and their places in society have changed considerably. The army of today seems more diffident than it was then, butchers' boys no longer carry the meat on their shoulders, and London weather must have been a great deal better for passengers to sit out on the top deck as they do here.

That's the Way to the Zoo: *Alfred Concanen*

THAT'S THE WAY TO THE ZOO.

WRITTEN & COMPOSED BY

J. F. MITCHELL.

SUNG WITH IMMENSE SUCCESS BY

T. W. BARRETT.

Despite his superb memory it is highly likely that Concanen used photographs as aids for certain details in his lithographs, including some of his portraits of music-hall artistes. Many celebrated artists have made use of the camera in this way; Frith had pictures taken at Epsom for his famous *Derby Day* painting and Concanen may well have used a photograph for the panoramic view on the cover of the *Grand Exhibition March*.

The Grand Exhibition of 1878 was probably the largest international exhibition that had ever been held up to that time. It was built on two large sites on either side of the River Seine in Paris. On one side was the Trocadéro and on the other were a number of smaller buildings and the Halles des Machines. The Trocadéro and the Palais de Champs-de-Mars were the permanent buildings that remained until 1937, when the Palais de Chaillot was erected for the exhibition that year and replaced the Trocadéro. After 1878 exhibitions were held in Paris at approximately 11-year intervals. The 1889 Exhibition centred around the newly erected Eiffel Tower.

Parisians may not recognize their city from Concanen's view but at the time London purchasers of this cover could obtain some idea of what was happening across the Channel. Concanen himself was a constant visitor to Paris.

Concanen used five stones to produce this picture and the technique required to fit these together as well as he has done was of the most advanced kind. So much had been packed into the drawing that a great deal of time can be spent simply working out what the Parisians in the picture are doing.

At one time the firm of Stannard and Dixon (later known as Stannard and Son), together with those of Hanhart and Packer, held a virtual monopoly in the printing of music covers. Some of the best illustrators were employed by Stannards—their artist-in-chief being Concanen himself. His name is as closely associated with Stannard and Dixon as, we shall later see, John Brandard's was with Hanhart.

During this period, Concanen also had his own printing works, first of all in partnership with Thomas Lee and later for a period with Siebe: some of the covers that we see now

Grand Exhibition March: *Alfred Concanen*

GRAND EXHIBITION MARCH.

CONCANEN LITH.

are signed 'Concanen, Lee and Siebe'. The premises of Stannard and Sons were at 7 Poland Street, London, right in the heart of the music-publishing industry. Great Marlborough Street adjoining Poland Street was then, and still is, a street for music publishers, and also houses the London College of Music.

In 1867, Novello, Ewer and Co. moved to Berners Street, London, W.1. where they were, with one exception, the only music publishers. Others soon followed. Eventually nineteen were to be found around these pioneers of cheap editions of good music. They carried on the business of publishing and lending rather like the tenants of Tin Pan Alley today.

All this suggests that Concanen's working world was confined to a small area. He lived at 43 Bloomsbury Street and virtually all his business connections could be reached on foot. In the evenings he could take a hansom cab to his beloved music-halls.

With his love of all things French, he must have been particularly charmed by Lecocq's operettas *La Fille de Madame Angot* and *Les Prés St Gervais.* One of Alexander Charles Lecocq's claims to fame was winning a prize awarded by Offenbach for his operetta *Le Docteur Miracle.* He shared the prize with Bizet. *Les Prés St Gervais* was produced in 1874 at the Criterion Theatre which had opened that year. The Criterion Theatre was considered very modern—it was built underground and air had to be pumped down to it.

Like the cover for *Madame Angot* this decidedly French scene suggests a light frothy plot with lots of Offenbach-like music. The expressions of the schoolboys and the teachers are worth noting; these were details that Concanen rarely missed. He has re-created the stage set used at the Criterion Theatre with all the atmosphere and immediacy possible. These two covers were works of his maturity and proved how well he had mastered his chosen technique.

Les Prés St Gervais: *Alfred Concanen*

Les PRÉS St. GERVAIS

QUADRILLE,
LECOCQ'S POPULAR COMIC OPERA
BY
ARBAN.

Price 4/-

London: ENOCH & SONS, 19, HOLLES St. CAVENDISH Sq W.

A much earlier cover by Concanen is *The Perfect Cure.*
This was produced in 1861 and protrays James Henry Stead
in the song which he made famous. The original was printed
in three colours. The costume consisted of plain red and
white vertical stripes with the usual brownish lithotint
background. It is deceptively simple in treatment, and the
stark figure suspended in mid-air rivets the attention of the
viewer. All extraneous detail has been omitted, and the
conical hat makes Stead appear ten feet tall.

Stead's performance of this song with its accompanying
dance was sensational. He was really a dancer and after
singing the verse and chorus he would leap up and down
over 400 times with both feet at once. According to a
contemporary magazine, *Household Words,* he could actually
perform this jump 1,600 times in succession.

During his short career Stead, like so many music-hall
artistes, appeared at three or four theatres in one evening,
performing the same act at each. This must have required
superhuman physical endurance, and the song was advertised as 'sung for upwards of nine hundred nights with
unbounded success' at Weston's Music Hall in Holborn.
Temporarily he achieved great fame in singing this song, but
his reputation soon afterwards dwindled into obscurity, and
in 1886 he died in an attic a poor man.

The spread of music-halls and their growing popularity
attracted over a period of years a number of American
troupes. The first of these was the Virginian Minstrels, who in
1843 appeared at the Adelphi Theatre in London. After a
moderately successful beginning, another troupe called *The
Etheopians* arrived on the scene. This troupe consisted of five
artistes and their refined performances were received
rapturously. A new style of entertainment soon became
firmly established. The effects of the Minstrels' arrival in
England are still to be seen, and even today such songs as
Swanee River and *Camptown Races* are sung.

The Negro Minstrel vogue started almost by accident. It
seems that Thomas Dartmouth Rice, an obscure American
actor, was walking along a main street in Cincinatti (there

Song of the Perfect Cure: *Alfred Concanen*

appears to be some doubt about the town) and saw a Negro street performer dancing and singing a song. The main chorus went:

Turn about and wheel about and do jes so,
An' every time I turn about I jump Jim Crow.

Rice was taken with this song and dance and soon afterwards (in Pittsburgh in 1830) he borrowed the ragged clothes of a Negro porter, appeared on the stage dressed in them and sang *Jim Crow.* He was an immediate sensation and when he had finished the song, the story goes, the porter who was worried about returning to work, came on stage and demanded his clothes back. The audience assumed this was part of the act and gave vent to even more enthusiastic applause. Perhaps the character of a Negro on the stage aroused the sympathy of the American public. The movement towards the emancipation of the slaves had started in the 1820s.

The best of Concanen's work was very fine, and his inherent good taste, first-class craftsmanship and versatility gave him an important place among his contemporaries. He did not aspire to great art but in his modest way he made a contribution to our records of Victorian history.

By the time that Alfred Concanen died, the new machine processes had almost completely taken over and the music covers had a 'new look' about them. The good taste and elegance which he and certain others had employed gave way to a more high-powered and commercial approach.

Rice pioneered the stage convention of a white man dressed as a Negro. Nobody could have visualized how far-reaching this was to become. Many years were to pass before a coloured actor actually appeared in a 'Nigger Minstrel' show. With the passage of time the term 'Jim Crow' took on less pleasurable connotations.

Alfred Concanen's cover for the minstrel song *Where's that Nigger Josey* shows the humour that so often appears in his work. He uses his skill as a cartoonist to distort the shapes of bodies and faces and produces a picture of the world that the minstrels created on the stage.

Where's that Nigger Josey?: *Alfred Concanen*

"WHERE'S THAT NIGGER JOSEY,"

OR,
THERE'LL BE NO FUN AT THE BALL TO NIGHT.

CHORUS. "Where has that nigger Josey gone?
Look for him everywhere,
There'll be no fun at the ball to night,
If Josey is'nt there,
There'll be no fun at the ball,
There'll be no fun at all,
There'll be no fun at the ball to night,
If Josey is'nt there."

WRITTEN BY

HARRY HUNTER,

COMPOSED BY *F. BULLEN,*
SUNG BY THE

MOHAWK MINSTRELS,
AGRICULTURAL HALL, LONDON.

Price 3/–

ENT. STA. HALL.

·LONDON;
HOPWOOD & CREW, 42, NEW BOND STREET, W.
STANNARD & SON, LITH?

Henry Maguire also came from an artistic family. He special-ized in full-length portraits of famous music-hall artistes, showing them as they appeared in their popular songs. He also made many woodcuts for magazines and 'penny dreadfuls' including *Alone in the Pirate's Lair* and *Broad Arrow Jack.*

His drawing of the minstrel banjoist A. G. White is beautiful by any standards. Perhaps lithography helps the translation of the drawing to the printed copy. There is no half-tone dot to break up the picture, so that the pencil strokes seem to be an actual original drawing. With lithographs from stone, as they were originally made before the camera came between the artist and the public, the grain of the stones faithfully reproduces the artist's intentions. Many artists have used the original method of lithography to ensure that prints of their pictures are faithful copies of their own handiwork, by drawing directly on to stone.

These pictures show the performers as they appeared on stage. The usual arrangement was for a group of five artistes to be seated in line. They were formally dressed in tailcoats, which appealed very much to English audiences, and provided a dignified family entertainment together with a new musical experience. The rhythmic Negro-style songs were completely different from any which had been heard in England before.

Rosa Lee: *Henry Maguire*

26

ROSA LEE.
OR DON'T BE FOOLISH JOE,

THE ONLY CORRECT AND AUTHORIZED EDITION OF
SONGS & MELODIES,
AS SUNG BY THE
ETHIOPIAN SERENADERS,
AT THE
ST JAMES'S THEATRE.

LONDON, PUBLISHED BY JOHN MITCHELL, PUBLISHER TO HER MAJESTY, 33, OLD BOND STREET.

Although the artist of *Down by the Riverside* is unknown, the cover is included because it is particularly appealing. The drawing is elegant and gentle. The song itself was a favourite of the Christy Minstrels, one of the most famous minstrel troupes. This idyllic illustration would have served equally well for the covers of many other songs, such as *Come Where My Love Lies Dreaming* or *Under the Willow She's Sleeping*.

There were special performances at Windsor for the Royal Family by various minstrel troupes. The vogue that these troupes created even spread to street performers who would set up their shows and perform to crowds in Regent Street and other main thoroughfares in the West End of London. In fact, the minstrels' influence has been so strong that B.B.C. Television's 'Black and White Minstrels' still retain stage conventions which originated 125 years ago.

Title page for
*Come Where My Love
Lies Dreaming*

Down by the River Side I Stray : *artist unknown*

28

SUNG BY
J. KAVANAGH OF THE MOHAWK MINSTRELS
(AGRICULTURAL HALL LONDON.)

DOWN BY THE RIVER SIDE I STRAY

COPYRIGHT

PRICE 3/-

BALLAD
WRITTEN BY
GEO. P. MORRIS
COMPOSED BY

J. R. THOMAS

FRANCIS BROS AND DAY (BLENHEIM HOUSE) 351 OXFORD ST W

No sector of life is overlooked by the music-cover illustrators. Politics, the army and navy, opera, ballet, royalty, sport, animals, landscapes, patriotism, and the music-hall—in fact most facets of life can be found in their work. This is their great fascination. The more covers that are seen, the more one realizes how wide is their coverage of the Victorian scene. These artists were true Victorians and they gloried in the eventful world in which they lived.

The colour and excitement of their own lives were often projected into their work and underlined their complete involvement in it. This was also acknowledged by the enormous public demand for their work. Concanen and Brandard were particularly famous. The music publishers actually advertised covers as having been drawn by them because they realized that this would promote sales, as shown overleaf.

If lithography had not been developed during this period, John Brandard almost certainly would have achieved fame as an artist anyway. He came from an artistic family, and his brother Robert was a noted engraver who exhibited frequently. He was born in 1812 and died in 1863. His life span covered the whole period during which hand lithography evolved and his contribution to the art of music-cover illustration was important. He used the most advanced contemporary ideas to obtain the effects he wanted to match his high aesthetic standards. He was a thoroughly trained artist with good taste although his drawings lacked vitality. The general approach of his work was highly finished and Brandard never used caricature or cartoon methods.

The *Cove of Cork* which illustrated this d'Albert composition is a leisurely, peaceful picture typical of Brandard's approach. The Irish scene, with its beautifully drawn sun on the sea and picnickers enjoying the view, has probably disappeared now along with the sailing boats.

Ireland : *John Brandard*

30

IRELAND

J. BRANDARD

The View of Cork

M & N. HANHART Imp.

QUADRILLE
UPON IRISH AIRS, BY
CHARLES D'ALBERT,

ENT. STA HALL

LONDON, CHAPPELL, 50 NEW BOND STREET

Above: One of A. W. Hammond's advertisements, featuring covers illustrated by various artists

Brandard was to the ballet and opera what Alfred Concanen later was to become to the 'lion comique' and music-hall. He illustrated stage scenes from operas and melodramas and usually chose a dramatic moment in the plot for his cover pictures.

The Corsican Brothers was one of the most celebrated of nineteenth-century melodramas. It was written by the Irish dramatist Dionysius Lardner Boucicault in 1852 and was first performed at the Princess's Theatre in London. Boucicault wrote about 150 plays, including translations and adaptations from novels. His first great success was *London Assurance,* a comedy originally seen at Covent Garden in 1841 with Madame Vestris, her husband Charles Mathews and William Farren in the principal roles. He followed this with many other successes and often appeared himself as an actor under the stage name of Lee Morton.

Perhaps the theme from the Corsican Brothers was a forerunner of theme music for the cinema. The melodramatic scene illustrated here is almost certainly what was seen in the

The Corsican Brothers : *John Brandard*

32

THE MELODY FROM
THE CORSICAN BROTHERS

ARRANGED BY

R. STÖPEL.

DIRECTOR OF THE MUSIC AT THE PRINCESS'S THEATRE

ENT. STA. HALL.

PRICE. 3/-

stage production. A subtly dramatic effect was achieved on the two-colour cover (shown here in monochrome) by using only one additional colour with the original black-and-white drawing. The brownish tint behind the drawing was eliminated in places to let light through, thus achieving the effect of stage lighting. The technique of colour lithography was evolving at the time yet this illustration could not have been improved by the addition of further colours.

Brandard took the greatest care in all his technical preparations to make the stones fit perfectly. He was lucky to work with the Hanharts, the famous firm of London lithographers, and together they formed a first-class team. Cost was not a major consideration and Brandard was given a free hand. His fee for a cover often reached 20 guineas, which by the standards of those days was an enormous amount. He was prolific and always employed two students or assistants to help him. Most of the covers executed by him were for music performed in the home, by the family at musical soirées, and thousands of pieces were written expressly for that purpose.

The average price for a cover was 3 shillings, in today's terms the equivalent of a pound. This indicates the prosperity of the Victorian music-publishing industry. It was, for instance, possible to sell 250,000 copies of the Myosotis waltz and the enormous revenue that this produced allowed the publishers to spend generously on illustrations for their covers.

Zuleika, Cellarius Valse and Mazurka is unmistakably by Brandard. He is more famous for his dancing scenes and ballet drawings than for anything else. This cover was drawn by Brandard himself as the annotation 'del. and lith.' implies. The couple illustrated seem, like so many of Brandard's dancers, to be idealized versions of Queen Victoria and Prince Albert. The elegant script at the foot of the drawing blends perfectly with the whole composition, while the delicate colouring should be noted; unlike so many of his contemporaries Brandard resisted the temptation to add unnecessary splashes of vivid colour.

Zuleika, Cellarius Valse and Mazurka: *John Brandard*

Zuleika,

Cellarius Valse & Mazurka.

Brandard loved ballet and spent a great deal of time studying dancers at work. He has been acknowledged as one of the most accurate portraitists of the famous ballerinas of his time. Degas was an admirer of his work and among the dancers Brandard portrayed were Charlotte Grisi, Fanny Cerrito and Marie Taglioni. These illustrations can be seen in the Marie Rambert collection at the Victoria and Albert Museum.

Like Alfred Concanen, John Brandard lived in great style. His imposing figure could often be seen at Drury Lane or Covent Garden, where he used to arrive in his own coach. His choice of friends and the subject-matter for his work was very cosmopolitan.

This lovely drawing of the Place de la Concorde in the *Paris Quadrille,* incidentally another d'Albert composition, gives an impression of Paris in the 1850s and '60s. On the right is the Ministre de la Marine, the French Admiralty, from which the Crown Jewels were stolen in 1792. On the left is the Hotel de Crillon, in which in 1778 France was the first country to recognize the independence of the United States. Between these two buildings runs the Rue Royale, at the end of which stands the famous church, the Madeleine.

It is not difficult to see why Brandard chose this square, which is one of the most beautiful in the world. Its perfect scale, with the eight stone pavilions, built in 1854, must have given the artist a very enjoyable subject. The Obelisk of Luxor in the centre is identical with that of Cleopatra's Needle in London, both of which were presented by Mohammed Ali. The two fountains are copies of those in the Piazza of St Peter's in Rome. Like all fountains in Paris, they play only on Sunday afternoons.

Paris Quadrille : *John Brandard*

PARIS

QUADRILLE

ON POPULAR FRENCH AIRS BY

CHARLES D'ALBERT.

LONDON, PUBLISHED BY CHAPPELL, MUSIC SELLER 50, NEW BOND ST.

When a song or piece of music was a best seller, the front cover often became 'debased' as the printers ran the covers off more quickly, eliminating the colours from the picture until they became a bare 'keystone' impression. Thus early and late impressions of the same cover may look like two entirely different pictures.

There are some beautiful black and white covers, the best of which are easily as attractive as the coloured examples. Many of the good artists in fact chose to work in black and white only.

When Brandard drew the cover for *The Bride's Farewell,* he gave a typical Victorian ballad a typical Victorian illustration, though the oval face and mouth are especially characteristic of Brandard's work. *The Bride's Farewell* must have been quite popular, as the cover was produced in a variety of states. It can be found in full colour, two or three colours, or in black and white only, like the specimen shown here.

John Brandard was one of the earliest and most skillful lithographic artists. During his lifetime lithography evolved from its tentative beginnings to a sophisticated and complicated industry. But in those days, the artist was a much more important figure in the process of producing an illustration than he is today. No tricks or gimmicks could cover a lack of technique, and until the advent of photography artists were valued very highly indeed by publishers.

When Brandard died in 1863, it was probably too early to see the effects of machine lithography which, undoubtedly in its early history, did not have the accuracy and finesse which the hand operators, personally supervised by the artists, seemed to possess. These artists were so directly involved in the finished work that each creation was a matter of personal pride. The comparative inaccuracy of the early machines, combined with the general lowering of artistic standards, shows clearly in the later Victorian covers.

The Bride's Farewell : *John Brandard*

THE BRIDE'S FAREWELL.

Set to Music by

JOHN BARNETT.

The cover opposite is in a style very similar to the faces of the *Zuleika* dancers and other Brandard portraits. Furthermore the illustration was printed by M. and N. Hanhart, his lithographers. These two factors strongly suggest that the artist was actually Brandard.

Cead Mille Failte! (Victoria and Erin Forever) is of great historical interest. It recorded the first visit to Ireland by a British monarch for 28 years. The Queen and Prince Consort regarded the visit more as a duty than a pleasure. In August 1847, after four disastrous years of famine, a temporary feeling of peace came to Ireland, and the Queen's advisers felt that it was an opportune moment for the Royal Family to make a State Visit. When the Queen, with her husband and the two eldest royal children arrived, they received a tumultuous reception which quite overwhelmed them. The crowds, as the picture shows, were particularly delighted to see the children, and the Prince of Wales was afterwards created Earl of Dublin.

The clothing, the decoration of the buildings and the attitude of the crowd tell the historian much about the event and the period. It is hard to believe that the artist would distort the scene in any serious way, though newspaper reports would probably induce him to add a certain amount of atmosphere.

The history of graphic work in the nineteenth century is really the story of the skill of its executants. There were no mechanical aids such as exist today and the most elaborate work was produced by hand.

Cead Mille Failte ! : *John Brandard*

The whole conception of the cover of *I Dream'd I saw a Garden Gay,* designed in the 1820s, is most beautifully thought out. Even if there were no illustration, the intricate and elegant wording would itself be sufficient to form a picture. Styles change, but this would be a typographic feast at any time. There are more than a dozen different typefaces used, yet they do not jar, and the balance is perfect. In later Victorian attempts at mixing typefaces, the effects were usually forceful but crude. They paved the way, however, for modern typographic display styles. Now that the older typefaces are coming back into fashion, we can appreciate even more the elegance of this early specimen.

Music publishers have proved to be extremely long-lived. Many firms which were operating 100 years ago are still prominent today, as, for example, Novello's, Boosey's, Chappell's, Francis Bros. & Day (Francis, Day and Hunter), and Hopwood and Crew (Ascherberg, Hopwood and Crew).

We know of no records that exist about the firm of W. and J. O. Clark in High Holborn, but this record of their skill deserves to be remembered.

One of the
decorative head pieces
used in *The Musical Bouquet*
series

I Dream'd I Saw a Garden Gay: *W. & J. O. Clark*

THIRD EDITION.

I DREAM'D I SAW A GARDEN GAY.

THE ADMIRED

Cavatina,

Sung by

MISS BRUCE & MISS LAND.

Mr. Robinson Mr. Bennett Mr. Land Mr. Anderson
also by

MR. HOBBS,

at the

Nobility's Concerts Festivals &c.

WRITTEN, COMPOSED & AFFECTIONATELY INSCRIBED

TO THE

Revd. John Malsbury Kirby.

by his Brother

W. KIRBY.

Ent. Sta. Hall. Pr. 2/-

Author of "The best Song that ever was Sung," "One little word my Love whisper'd to me," "My Helen is the Fairest Flower," "The Beautiful Eye," &c. &c.

LONDON.

Mori & Lavenu, 28, New Bond Street, Allcroft, 15, New Bond Street, Oventry & Hollier, 71, Dean Street, Soho. Crammer Addison, & Beale Regent Street. Bruce Hanway St. G. Platt, 9, John St. Oxford St. T.C. Bates, 6, Ludgate Hill. J. Turner, 64 Leadenhall St. and by all the principal Music Sellers in the United Kingdom.

The first music covers were printed with the title of the music on the front. Later the fancy border design or an engraved vignette printed from a copper plate appeared on many music sheets. Etching was succeeded by the woodcut, then by steel engraving. Also used were the mezzotint, stipple and aquatint.

The Citizen Galop, the music of which was composed by Carl Volti, is a Scottish contribution. This Glasgow street-scene is a pleasing, tastefully executed picture by an unknown artist and tells us something of society at that time. Barefoot children are on the streets selling newspapers, while one child does somersaults to amuse passers-by. We can also see how pianos were moved a century ago.

Title page to Montgomery's
Blow, Bugle, Blow

The Citizen Galop: *artist unknown*

44

THE
CITIZEN GALOP

LONDON PIANO-FORTE & MUSIC SELLER

BY

CARL VOLTI.

ENT: STA: HALL.

PRICE 4.

EDINBURGH
ALL MUSIC-SELLERS.

GLASGOW,

LONDON
CHAPPELL & C.

One of the most memorable events in England in the nineteenth century was the Great Exhibition of 1851. Prince Albert, who was the driving force behind it, showed a keen interest in all technical innovations. All the prominent printers vied with each other to show the best examples of their craft and, as lithographic art was at its peak, this was an excellent opportunity for printers and artists to produce a record of all the buildings and exhibits.

Many music covers of the Crystal Palace were produced. George Madeley printed the *Quadrille of all Nations* at his press in Wellington Street, Strand. The Crystal Palace was an enormous structure, over 1800 feet long, 456 feet wide and 66 feet high. The floor area of more than 800,000 square feet housed over 15,000 exhibitors. The 11 miles of tables showed over £2,000,000 worth of goods which were seen by more than 5,000,000 people. The Royal Family were frequent visitors.

Madeley's detailed drawing of the Art Palace is still very rewarding to look at today. The various figures in national dress show the first mass tourist descent into England which the Exhibition created.

The half-title, examples of which are shown on pages 26, 28, 42 and 44, was often used for a series of publications. This sort of title introduced songs by popular composers like Stephen Foster and W. H. Montgomery. *The Musical Bouquet* was a regular series of publications published by J. Bingly and W. Strange from 1846 to 1889, and during its lifetime over 5,000 pieces of music were produced under this heading. Many of the finest black and white titles were in this series, printed either by engraving or by lithography.

Another series, *The Queen's Boudoir* issued in 1841 by Nelson and Jeffreys, which was first designed by Brandard and printed by the Hanharts, saw the introduction of colour lithography into music covers. This series had a high standard of artistry and production, and was the begininning of the rise in quality which eventually produced a great flowering of talent.

There were other important personalities concerned in the

Quadrille of all Nations: *George Madeley*

46

QUADRILLE OF ALL NATIONS

ART PALACE.
(HYDE PARK)

INTRODUCING 21 NATIONAL MELODIES

Composed & Dedicated

TO

THE MISSES SHARWOOD

BY

W. WILSON.

Ent. Sta. Hall.   *Price 3/*

London: Published by T. E. PURDAY, 50 S.t Pauls Ch.Yd.

development of illustrated music covers before and around this time and mention must be made of Louis Antoine Jullien. Actually he had no less than thirty-six Christian names. His father was a violinist playing with the Philharmonic Society at the time of his baptism, and asked one of the members of the orchestra to act as a godfather. All thirty-six players insisted on being godfathers and giving the baby their own Christian names.

He came to London from France in 1838 and in a comparatively short while became well known as a conductor and arranger of music. In fact his promenade concerts were a feature of London musical life. In 1843 he became a music publisher and opened a shop in Maddox Street. Within a year he had agencies in many of the capital cities of Europe. Jullien employed some of the best artists—including John Brandard —and the covers produced for him were often forerunners in style and conception. His standards of music publishing were consistently high, but when Covent Garden Opera House was burnt down he lost most of his stock of covers. This seemed to be a breaking point for him and he died a few years later in a mental home in his native France.

Working at the same time as Alfred Concanen, but in a different style, was Thomas Packer. His specialities were highly-coloured landscapes, brilliantly-hued skies and sunset and moonlight effects. Packer ran a large studio, and during his career employed many apprentices who afterwards themselves became prominent in the same field. Often Packer did not bother to sign his own work, but his unique style is usually recognizable.

His cover for *The Great International Exhibition Quadrille,* published in 1862, is charming and elegant. Although Packer was best known for highly-coloured effects, this cover shows great restraint in its subtle use of shade and is a lovely drawing.

Packer was an innovator in lithography. He devised his own technique for coloured effects and earned from his artist colleagues—with whom he was a popular figure—the title of 'The Graduated-Tint Packer'. So many of them had started

Great International Exhibition Quadrille: *Thomas Packer*

GREAT
INTERNATIONAL EXHIBITION

QUADRILLE,
BY
J. PRIDHAM.

LONDON, GEORGE EMERY & C? 408, OXFORD STREET.
JUST PUBLISHED,

ENT. STA. HALL.

PRICE 3

under his supervision that he must be regarded as a very important figure in the field of music illustration.

He drew this cover for the *Streets of London Quadrilles* from the Trafalgar Square end of St Martin's Lane. St Martin's-in-the-Fields Church is on the left and beyond can be seen the Square much as it is today. The view is, however, very much distorted as St Martin's Place in fact lies at a completely different angle. The small police box with the lamp above was often referred to as the 'smallest police station in England'. The 'Peelers'—forerunners of our policemen—are keeping a stern watch on the activities around them.

The illustration was based on a scene from the musical extravaganza *The Streets of London* by T. Westrop, which ran successfully at the now defunct Princess's Theatre in the 1860s. The production was one of Charles Hall's many operetta triumphs and is now mainly remembered for its spectacular fire scene. The same play was produced in America as *The Poor of New York,* in the Boulevard Theatre in Paris as *Les Pauvres de Paris,* at the Strand Theatre in London as *Pride and Poverty,* at Sadler's Wells as *The Poor of Islington* or *Life in the Street,* and in Liverpool as *The Poor of Liverpool!*

The Princess's in London was one of Queen Victoria's favourite theatres. It was here that melodrama played to packed houses and the Queen was seen to clutch the curtain of her box in terror when a murderer in the plot had the beautiful heroine in his grasp.

This winter scene (somewhat reminiscent of a stage set for *La Bohème*) tells us more about the West End of London 100 years ago than any written description. Packer has produced one of his highly-coloured skies here, but although it is mid-winter the feeling is a happy one.

In many of the songs of this period the words have no merit at all, but one of the songs from the *Streets of London* has a

Streets of London Quadrilles: *Thomas Packer*

50

marvellously colourful refrain which describes the first impressions made on a new arrival in London:

> *Selling off at prime cost,*
> *Watches, chains, and seals lost,*
> *Ord'nary ev'ry day at one*
> *Carpets beat, and Porter's work done,*
> *The original coffee mart,*
> *Goods removed with horse and cart,*
> *Instruments tun'd, and let on hire,*
> *Barclay Perkin's and Co's entire,*
> *Music provided, dancing taught,*
> *Old irons, rags, and phials bought,*
> *Ladies ears pierc'd with ease,*
> *Butter, bacon, eggs and cheese,*
> *Married women run away,*
> *Muffins and crumpets twice a day,*
> *Evening paper taken in,*
> *Jamaica Rum and Hodge's Gin,*
> *Burton, Alsop's Bass's Ale,*
> *Notorious fraud, the last day's sale,*
> *Money lent cent per cent,*
> *Dollars bought, music taught.*

The magnificent cover for *God Bless the Prince of Wales* was designed by Packer for a song which for some time had its place among the patriotic songs of England. In the British Museum library alone there are listed over thirty-five versions written for choirs, schools, instrumental ensembles, orchestras etc. It was originally written in 1862 and became a semi-national anthem in Wales. In 1867 the composer was presented to Prince Edward, afterwards Edward VII, who had been made Prince of Wales a month after he was born. Prince Edward married Princess Alexandra, a daughter of the King of Denmark, on 10 March 1863, and the wedding ceremony took place in St George's Chapel, Windsor. This cover was published at the same time. The window illustrated here is no longer in existence. It was altered late in 1863 and unveiled by Queen Victoria as a memorial to the Prince Consort.

God Bless the Prince of Wales: *Thomas Packer*

GOD BLESS THE PRINCE OF WALES,

Spearman

(THE NEW NATIONAL SONG.)
COMPOSED & ARRANGED FOR THE
PIANO FORTE,
BY
BRINLEY RICHARDS.

LONDON; ROBERT COCKS & Co. NEW BURLINGTON STREET W.
BY SPECIAL APPOINTMENT.

ENT. STA. HALL.
COPYRIGHT

Piano Solo 4/-
Piano Duet 4/-
Song 3/-

This picture of upper- and middle-class society at the Vauxhall Gardens gives us some idea of the scale of that famous entertainment centre. Packer's *Al Fresco* portrays the bandstand and shows the lighting effects which were a feature of the gardens and helped to draw large crowds for so long.

The Vauxhall Gardens began as a place of pleasure in the seventeenth century when Sir Samuel Morland built a mansion there. Concerts were given and Charles II used to visit the house accompanied by various lady friends.

In the eighteenth century, Dr Johnson, who frequently visited the gardens, described them as 'a curious show, gay exhibition, music vocal and instrumental, not too refined for the general ear, for all of which only a shilling is paid'. Boswell mentions them in his *Life of Samuel Johnson* and among other visitors were Pepys, Horace Walpole, Sir Joshua Reynolds, Dickens, Thackerary, Macaulay and Leigh Hunt. Hogarth, who was a friend of Thomas Tyers, the son of the subsequent proprietor, was given a gold ticket of admission in perpetuity for himself and his friends in return for some pictures he painted for the gardens. This ticket was handed down to Hogarth's descendents.

The entertainment in the gardens began in the spring and continued until the autumn. A fairyland of illuminated walks and fireworks displays were arranged, and these attracted family parties who could be sure of seeing royalty and high society, whom they acknowledged with great applause.

The best entertainers, such as Madame Vestris, were employed, and they attracted very large audiences. Another attraction which became a popular feature was ballooning. Frequent ascents were made and distances of up to 50 miles were covered.

Lithography, with which we are mainly concerned, was invented in 1793 by Senefelder, who introduced it into England. It took time to achieve popularity in a country which was slow in general to adopt new methods, but eventually lithography became the chief medium for music illustration.

Al Fresco: *Thomas Packer*

By the 1820s the process was firmly established. Engelman started business in London in 1826 and eventually new firms set up in print. Machines, introduced in 1850, were at first very primitive and the period 1840-1860 was the golden age of hand lithography. There was plenty of work, the artists were well paid and there was not much competition. This music-publishing industry used lithographed music covers in the same way that record sleeves are used today. The history of music illustration could be regarded as the history of lithography in England.

The feelings of our forefathers about patriotism, war and the British Empire can be gauged by the songs that they sung. *Who'll Fight For The Queen* by George Linley, who wrote *God Bless the Prince of Wales,* struck a responsive chord in his compatriots. This appeared in the period which produced *Sons of the Sea,* the unique *We Don't Want To Fight, But By Jingo If We Do,* which was sung by the Great Macdermott, who as a result of specializing in these patriotic songs became known as 'The Statesman of the Halls'.

This cover was designed by Augustus 'Gus' Butler, another of the artists in the Stannard and Dixon stable, for whom he worked exclusively. Even amongst his fellow artists, he was considered Bohemian. His range of work was very wide, but he seemed to prefer military subjects and was rumoured to have been a soldier at one time. He did not work spontaneously, but had to work up a drawing laboriously, although this did not detract from its liveliness. Always a *bon viveur,* his liking for hip flasks and petticoats was well known.

The picture shows a recruiting station with the campaign in full swing. The officer in the centre is urging the country lad to join and at the rear on the right, a recruiting sergeant seems to have succeeded. The 'Increased Bounty' notice on the wall was a big factor in recruiting. When times were prosperous and the army needed men, the bounty was increased; when times were bad and employment was short the bounty, usually paid in golden guineas, fell to nothing.

Who'll Fight for the Queen? : *Augustus Butler*

WHO'LL FIGHT FOR THE QUEEN?

WRITTEN AND COMPOSED BY

GEORGE LINLEY.

LONDON.

ENT. STA. HALL

Pr. 2/6

The visit of their Royal
Highnesses the Prince of
Wales and Prince Alfred to
Messrs. Day and Son, 1856

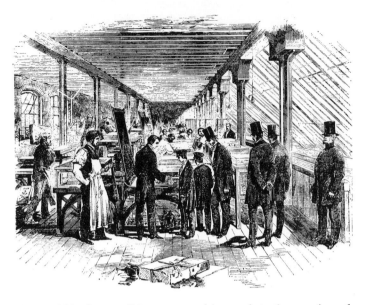

It would be impossible to state with certainty the number of
music covers produced, but it was definitely more than
80,000. In Victorian times they were not regarded as having
any intrinsic value, and consequently many have disappeared
forever.

Prince Albert, who had had a very good musical education,
composed many songs, chorales, and ballads. Queen Victoria
is reputed to have been so charmed by the covers that she had
a small press installed in the palace to print covers for the
royal children. They actually visited a factory in 1856, and
The Times on May 3rd of that year reported:

'On Tuesday week, their Royal Highnesses the Prince of
Wales and Prince Alfred, accompanied by Mr Gibbs, Dr
Becker and Colonel Biddulph, honoured the establishment
of Messrs Day & Son, lithographers to the Queen, with a
visit, in order to inspect the progress of the many important
works on chromo-lithography now being produced by this
eminent firm'.

The name 'Rotten Row' is said to have originated from the
French *Route Du Roi.* Rotten Row is a riding track which runs
for over a mile through Hyde Park and has been a fashionable
rendezvous for horsemen for more than 300 years.

Hyde Park was opened to the public by Charles II in 1660

Rotten Row Galop: *artist unknown*

ROTTEN ROW GALOP.

FOR THE PIANO-FORTE. COMPOSED BY

and from that time has been a favourite playground for Londoners. During its history it has seen duellists, highwaymen, political agitators and all manner of sporting events.

The unknown artist shows Victorian high society as it must have appeared in 1853 when this cover was first published. Whole families obviously enjoyed dressing up to ride in Rotten Row.

The Times Galop is an example, not of artistry, but of the early use of modern advertising techniques.

The date on this cover is 1853, but it would not be out of place in the 1960s. The copywriter uses each classified advertisement to 'push' the publisher's list of music. This was a real 'hard sell' and an especially striking cover was very often used to sell inferior music. The use of *The Times* headline in the music title shows that the Editor was not adverse to publicity.

This is a fascinating cover, humourous and entertaining. The music has long been forgotten, but the cover is sufficiently original to be remembered for its own sake.

The appeal of the covers as works of art has only recently begun to emerge, owing to the persistence of a few dedicated enthusiasts. Their charm has immediate appeal, and an ever-growing number of collectors now look for them avidly.

Carl Maria von Weber and his father were among the first to employ lithography for music printing. Weber's early works were printed from stone to save the expense of engraved plates. When Weber's first composition failed for a time he abandoned music as a career for lithography. His success in 1804 with *Rubezahl* made him return to music.

Weber nearly died as a result of accidentally drinking some nitric acid used in lithography. The bottle was left on the table by his father, and Weber, thinking it was wine, drunk the contents. His mouth and throat were badly burned, it took over two months for him to recover and his voice was permanently affected.

The Times Galop: *artist unknown*

STEAM to INDIA.—HENRY DISTIN begs to inform the Commanding Officers and Presidents of Band Committees of Her Majesty's Army and Navy and the Hon. East India Company, that he has made arrangements with several of the East India Agents to supply them with Instruments at his own Manufactory for Military Bands, and all orders he may be favoured with through them, or otherwise, will be punctually attended to, and forwarded by Steam or Sailing Vessels with the greatest care and attention.

IF THIS SHOULD MEET THE EYE of Amateur Cornet Players, they are earnestly requested to call at H. Distin's Manufactory, Leicester Square, London, and inspect the great improvements H. Distin has made in all kinds of Brass Instruments.

LION GALOP, for Pianoforte and Cornet. Published by Henry Distin, 31 Cranbourn Street, Leicester Square. Price 3s.

CALIFORNIA.—NOTICE to SHIPPERS.—An excellent opportunity is now offered to Merchants for supplying Military Musical Instruments manufactured by Henry Distin, Cranbourn Street, Leicester Square, London. Conditions of sale may be known on application.

PEASANT POLKA—as performed by the Hungarian Band, with unbounded applause, and nightly encored. Published for Pianoforte and Cornet by H. Distin. Sent post free, price 2s. 6d.

DISTIN'S MILITARY BAND INSTRUMENTS. Before purchasing Military Musical Instruments, obtain Lists of Prices and Drawings, and Testimonials from various Regiments of the superiority of Instruments manufactured by Henry Distin, 31 Cranbourn Street, Leicester Square, London.

CHRISTMAS PRESENTS.—What handsomer present could you send to your friend in the country than a hamper containing one of Distin's Saxhorns, a pair of Cymbals, and a copy of the "Times Galop?" 31 Cranbourn Street, Leicester Sq.

TIMES GALOP, by KALOZDY, arranged for the Pianoforte, with Cornet Accompaniment, price 3s., as performed by the Hungarian Band at the Marionette Theatre, under the direction of KALOZDY—nightly encored. Published by Henry Distin, Military Musical Instrument Maker, 31 Cranbourn Street, Leicester Square, London.

MAGYAR WAR MARCH, for Pianoforte and Cornet. Price 3s. 6d. Sent post free, from H. Distin.

QUEEN'S HUSSAR—Galop, by J. P. Clark, published by H. Distin, for Pianoforte and Cornet. Sent post free, price 3s.

SALON QUADRILLE, for Pianoforte and Cornet. Price 3s. Sent post free.

MAZURKA HEROIQUE, for Pianoforte and Cornet. Price 3s. 6d. Sent post free, from H. Distin.

KALOZDY'S MUSIC AS A PRESENT (£1 1s.)—Eleven of the most popular pieces, as performed by the Hungarian Band, bound in cloth, with likeness of Kalozdy, drawn by Baugniet, and full length portraits in colours of the Performers, carriage free, from Henry Distin, Military Musical Instrument Maker, and sole Publisher of Kalozdy's Dance Music, 31 Cranbourn-street, Leicester square, London.

DRUMS, THE LARGEST STOCK in LONDON.—Manufactured by H. Distin on a new principle. Drawings and explanations sent post free from the Depôt, 31 Cranbourn-street, Leicester square, London.

DISTIN'S PATENT CORNETS, ALTHORNS, EUPHONIUMS, &c., manufactured by H. Distin, under his direction, and of the same class as those performed on by the Distins at their Concerts, which have received her Majesty's and His Royal Highness Prince Albert's highest approbation; also the entire approval of every Regiment that H. Distin has had the honour of serving. The following is a copy of a letter from the President of the Band Committee of the 17th Lancers.

CONSTANTINOPLE.—Cymbals of the largest and finest quality may be had of H. Distin, 31 Cranbourn Street, Leicester Square, London.

TIBER—Waltz, by Farrugia, published by H. Distin, for Pianoforte and Cornet. Sent post free, price 3s.

"To Mr H. Distin.—Sir,—I think it but right to inform you that the whole of the Instruments you supplied to us are highly approved of, and have given us every satisfaction. Major Willet, F.R.C.

A complete List of Prices and Drawings of 40 different kinds of Instruments, with opinions of the public press, and Testimonials from various Regiments in her Majesty's service, may be had free from H. Distin, 31 Cranbourn-street, Leicester-square, London.

No. 10. Distin's Military Cornet, (by this arrangement the Cornet is made smaller, the springs being placed at the bottom of the pistons,) in B flat, with crooks down to G flat, fitted in a strong case, complete, £8 8s.

DO YOU BRUISE YOUR OATS?—No; but we sometimes bruise our Cornets, and we take them to Distin, 31 Cranbourn Street, Leicester Square.

THE GREAT GLOBE is in Leicester Square, close to Cranbourn Street, where H Distin always keeps a large stock of Musical Instruments on hand.

This Cornet is well adapted for Military Bands, being every portable, and extremely easy in producing the high notes; and it is also made in C, with crooks down to G.
Bard Masters of first-rate ability provided for Regiments.

FIRE! FIRE! FIRE!—A complete blaze of triumph is nightly achieved at the Royal Marionette Theatre, by the performance of the "Times Galop," published by H. Distin, 31 Cranbourn Street, Leicester Square.

AUSTRALIA.—HENRY DISTIN begs to inform his Patrons in Australia, that he has now completed most extensive Alterations and Improvements in his Manufactory, by the addition of the finest Machinery, on the most approved principles, and engaged the best Workmen in London and Paris, and is now enabled, with greater facility, to manufacture every article connected with Military Musical Instruments,—which, being made under his immediate direction, are proved and tuned by himself, he being a Performer and Professor on Brass Instruments; it must therefore be obvious, he has an advantage over many manufacturers who are unable to do so, all orders for Instruments to be addressed to his Manufactory, 31 Cranbourn Street, Leicester Square, London.

DISTIN'S JOURNAL, for Cornet and Pianoforte. Published in 12 Numbers, 3s. 6d. each, sent post free; or the whole of the 12 Numbers bound, for £1 1s.

NEXT OF KIN—Wanted, a Galop that shall be at all akin to the "Times Galop," published by H. Distin, 31 Cranbourn Street, Leicester Square.

DUKE OF CAMBRIDGE'S Quick March, by Schallen, price 3s. Published for Cornet and Pianoforte, by H. Distin. Sent post free.

THE NORTH-WEST PASSAGE from St. Martin's Lane to Leicester Square, leads directly in front of H. Distin's Musical Instrument Warehouse, 31 Cranbourn Street.

MALTA.—Quadrille, by KALOZDY, price 3s. 6d. The celebrated Malta Quadrille, as performed by the Hungarian Band under the direction of the Author, at the Marionette Theatre, London. Post free, 3s. 6d.

DISTIN'S TUTOR, price 6s., for Cornet, Althorn, and Tenor Tuba, and on the Art of Single and Double Tonguing. Published by H. Distin, 31 Cranbourn Street, London.

IF the GENTLEMAN WHO LEFT HIS HOME in consequence of being constantly tormented by his wife's performance of trashy music, will return to his affectionate family, he will find that every thing has been arranged to his satisfaction, the lady having resolved to play nothing but KALOZDY's Music for the future.

PARIS.—An Arrangement having been entered into by H. Distin with the largest Parisian Manufacturers of Musical Instruments, the Public can now be supplied with Cornet-à-Pistons for beginners at £1 3s. up to £5 5s. A large stock always on hand at 31 Cranbourn Street, Leicester Square, London.

VICTORIEN POLKA, for Pianoforte and Cornet. Price 3s. 6d. Sent post free.

THE MOST INTERESTING GROUP ever modelled is the Group of CORNETS in Henry Distin's window, 31 Cranbourn Street.

NIAGARA—Waltz, by Schallehn, published by H. Distin for Pianoforte and Cornet. Sent post free, price 3s.

ASCENT of MONT BLANC.—If you do go up Mont Blanc, be sure to take one of Distin's Sax-horns with you. You will not regret doing this. 31 Cranbourn Street, Leicester Square.

TO THE EMBARRASSED.—Persons of limited means who are in doubt as to what Music they ought to purchase, will find the best collection at Distin's.

THIRD DRAGOON GUARDS.—Waltz, by Rumgeling. Published by H. Distin for Pianoforte and Cornet. Sent post free, price 3s.

CLOSURE OF BETTING HOUSES. IMPORTANT!—The only "Galop" of the day on which it is legitimate to bet is the "Times," success is sure to follow—to find a better is impossible.

ILKA QUADRILLE, for Pianoforte and Cornet. Price 3s. 6d. Sent post free.

THE sixt heb estgal lopth atev crwasw. ritteno rarren ged. publi abeth, phen epda lheran hos estelo atdelc setersu satve. Dec. 1853.

IMPORTANT TO LADIES. HABITS!—These should be of the best whether in cloth or music. In Music ladies should acquire the habit of playing those pieces which are best suited to the occasion. They will find the "Times Galop" the best of its kind.

OUR POLKA.—By Beresford, Published for Pianoforte and Cornet, by H. Distin. Sent post free, price 3s. 6d.

LOST; the peace of mind of half the young ladies in London, ever since they heard Kalozdy's new Times Galop. Whoever will restore the same to their owners shall receive a copy of the Galop as a reward for their trouble.

NOTICE. Any Gentleman or Lady calling at the Royal Marionette Theatre, any evening between the hours of 8 and 11, will be certain to hear something to their advantage.

CUCKOO GALOP—Published for the Pianoforte and Cornet by H. Distin. Sent post free, price 3s.

CADOGAN POLKA—by Kalozdy. Just Published by Henry Distin, for Pianoforte and Cornet, price 3s. 6d.

EMMA is earnestly entreated to return to her disconsolate parents. All the past shall be forgiven, and in future she shall be allowed to play the "Times Galop" all day long if she is disposed to do so.

MISSING, a gentleman about 20 years of age, of middle height, and acute sensibilities. Last seen in the neighbourhood of Cranbourn Street; it is supposed that on hearing Kalozdy's new "Times Galop he was so affected that he has ever since been of unsound mind.

CORNET DUETTS, NEW SERIES of TWELVE.—Cornet Duetts by Bausain, in six numbers 1s. 6d. each number containing two Duetts in each, or the whole bound together, price 15s. Published by Henry Distin, 31 Cranbourn-street, Leicester square, London.

STANNARD & DIXON, 7 POLAND ST.

Composed & Arranged for the Piano Forte,
BY
KALOZDY

AND PERFORMED BY THE HUNGARIAN BAND AT THE MARIONETTE THEATRE.

LONDON, PUBLISHED BY H. DISTIN, MILITARY MUSICAL INSTRUMENT MANUFACTORY.

Another executant was Alexander Laby (1814-1899), whose subjects were often of a serious or religious nature. He worked only spasmodically, as his highly strung temperament often put him out of action.

Although he produced a large number of titles, S. Rosenthal never regarded this as his main occuptaion, but it is evident from his music covers that he was a very refined lithographic artist. He was also a printer.

Alfred Bryan (1852-1899) was a skilled caricaturist in black and white. He had a remarkable facility for making quick sketches of his subjects and could then work up a life-like portrait from memory. He found this ability to be of considerable value for stage portraits.

This philatelic specimen, *Polka des Timbres Poste* is another example of the use of ephemera, like the *Times Galop* on the previous page. The approach of the artist here is modern : instead of portraying the subject pictorially he has used the stamps to form a geometrical pattern.

Senefelders adaptation of the rolling press, 1818

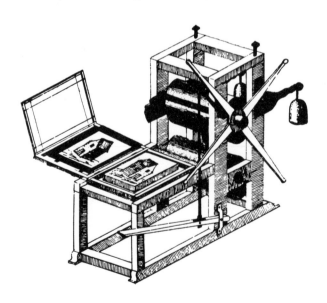

Polka des Timbres Poste : *artist unknown*

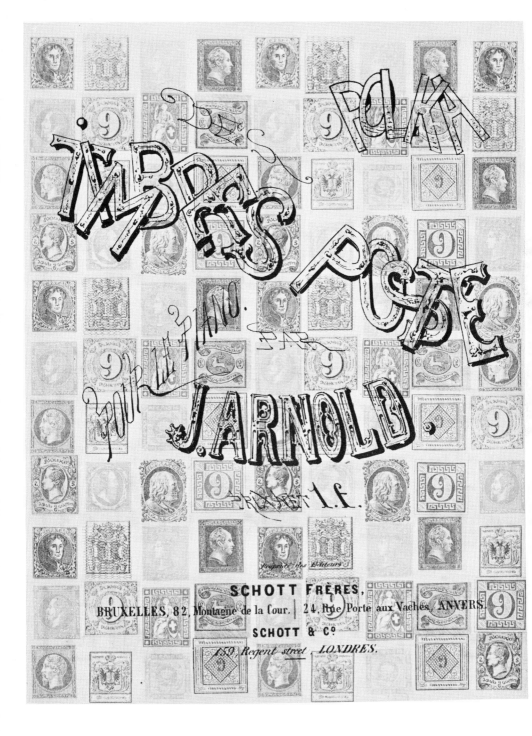

Other famous artists produced music covers. Toulouse Lautrec is known to have done some in France; Gordon Craig, the great stage designer and innovator and son of Ellen Terry, designed covers at a later date; and George Cruickshank was working for music publishers in London in the mid-nineteenth century. This cover for *Fairy Songs and Ballads for the Young* by Cruickshank shows that the young in those days were used to a diet of strong meat. Each of the panels depicts one of the songs in the book. The stories themselves, like many fairy tales of that time, were often gruesome and Cruickshank's drawings are very realistic. Whether his work is liked or not, he is undoubtedly among the greatest of English illustrators. He was born in 1792 in Bloomsbury and in the 1820s he was already well known as a cartoonist and political satirist with no respect for the Establishment. As 'Phiz' in *Punch,* he became a household name. Although during his long life the style of humorous art changed constantly he managed to remain at the top of his profession.

'Phiz' was known throughout his long life for his great energy, even at the age of 80. He died in 1878 at the age of 86. Of all the cover artists he was the only one to achieve widespread fame, although in a more general field than that of music illustration.

Cruickshank's main work was in book and magazine illustration, a medium more durable than music covers. Perhaps if others had worked in this field, their names would have become better known.

This style of cover with small panels developed in the 1840s and in this case the publisher was D'Almaine. He and Jullien ran the two houses producing the best covers. They commissioned work by the best artists and did a great deal to establish a high general standard.

Fairy Songs and Ballads: *George Cruikshank*

FAIRY
SONGS & BALLADS
For the Young.

Written, Composed
and
Dedicated
To
Her Royal Highness
The PRINCESS ROYAL

BY
O. B. DUSSEK.

In Two Books Price 4s each Book
London   F.S.H
D'Almaine & Co: 20 Soho Square

George Cruikshank.

Hundreds of composers were constantly producing new works for an insatiable public. The rise of the middle classes, with a resulting increase of musical education at home, produced a new generation of daughters who could play the piano and sing or accompany the rest of the family. Although this strata of society rarely ventured into public places of entertainment, the popular songs were still sung in their homes.

The Lost Child is the only example in this collection of an engraving. As a picture of a melodramatic scene, it is full of action and atmosphere. The face of the half-crazed woman stands out from the set expressions of the rest of the crowd. Life goes on with a Punch and Judy show in the background. The style in which only part of the page is used for the illustrations is characteristic of earlier music titles.

The unknown artist must have been in quite a quandary as to how to depict this 'comic' song. Fortunately the woman finds her child in the last verse. Thomas Hood (1799-1845), the lyricist of *The Lost Child,* was famous as a writer of verse and as an editor of periodicals such as the *Gem,* the *New Monthly Magazine* and *Hood's Magazine,* for all of which he wrote mainly humorous material. He was one of the earliest contributors to *Punch* and numbered De Quincey, Hazlitt and Charles Lamb amongst his friends. In 1844 Hood developed consumption, became too ill to work and was given a pension by Sir Robert Peel.

From the 1820s onwards, lithography began to replace engravings for music illustration. In those early days English style was very much influenced by the French, as is shown by *The Lost Child* with the title above the vignette and lettering below. Eventually the picture became larger until it occupied the whole page.

A very different street scene was drawn by Frank Trevisany, an artist who flourished much later. He was born in 1840 and came to England from Bavaria in 1860. He drew a number of covers of comic singers and also many covers for the *Musical Bouquet.*

The Lost Child: *artist unknown*

THE LOST CHILD,

The admired Comic Song.

SUNG AT Public Concerts BY

Mr GEORGE FORD.

The Words by

THOMAS HOOD.

LONDON:
MUSICAL BOUQUET OFFICE, 192, HIGH HOLBORN;
& J. ALLEN, 20, WARWICK LANE, PATERNOSTER ROW.

Nº 803, MUSICAL BOUQUET.

The *Burlington Waltz* cover, published in 1871, shows one of the most elegant shopping arcades in London. From the day it was built in 1819 it prospered. It was part of the Burlington House site and attracted the *haut monde* from the very beginning. Both men and women could find clothes in the very latest fashion. All the trappings of affluent life were to be seen in the fifty-five shops that existed in 1828. It has altered slightly over the years but still remains much the same as when it was first built. Trevisany's over-elaborate *pot-pourri* still manages to be elegant and to convey the atmosphere in which the leisured classes lived.

Towards the end of the nineteenth century the standards of musical illustration started to decline. Colour was crudely used and photographic aids were beginning to oust the illustrator and to reduce him to the level of a technician. It is necessary to return to the early days to seek the refinement that had disappeared.

Maxim Gauci (1774-1854) has often been called 'the father of music-title artists'. He started painting miniatures in Paris, and Napoleon commissioned him to paint eight miniatures of himself which he presented to various kings and queens of Europe. Before the Battle of Waterloo his family came to England, where he found plenty of opportunity as a lithographic artist. His titles appeared from 1815-1850. They form a unique record and show many characteristics of that period. He did several portraits of Miss Love (afterwards the Countess of Harborough). Also from Gauci we have many portraits of the famous Madame Vestris.

The legendary 'Madame' was born in Dean Street, Soho. She made her first appearance in 1815 at the King's Theatre, afterwards Her Majesty's. She also sang Italian opera at Covent Garden, the Haymarket and Drury Lane, where her lovely contralto voice and great personal beauty made her the idol of audiences. She managed Covent Garden with her second husband from 1839-1842. Her appearances as a popular singer at the Vauxhall Gardens and various concert halls guaranteed full houses. As a singer, she preferred the songs and ballads of the popular theatre to the more demand-ing roles of the operatic stage. Her songs included *Cherry*

The Burlington Waltz: *Frank Trevisany*

THE BURLINGTON WALTZ,

BURLINGTON

BY
HENRY PARKER.

LONDON: PUBLISHED BY C. SHEARD, MUSICAL BOUQUET OFFICE, 192. HIGH HOLBORN.

CITY WHOLESALE AGENTS; E. W. ALLEN, II. AVE. MARIA LANE; & F. PITMAN, 20. PATERNOSTER ROW.

Nos 4546 & 4547. Musical Bouquet.

ENTERED AT STATIONERS' HALL

Ripe, Rise Gentle Moon, Oysters Sir and *Buy a Broom,* which referred to the Bavarian girls who could often be seen in the streets of London selling their wares.

Gauci drew this charming cover portraying Madame Vestris in one of her most famous songs. The music of the first published edition of *Buy a Broom* was written by Sir Henry Bishop, famous as the composer of *Home Sweet Home.* His enormous output included operas, dramas and ballads. James Robinson Planche wrote the original words. On the cover featuring Madame Vestris, neither the original composer nor the lyricist appear. The publisher has also changed. It seems that there were several Bavarian girls' songs arranged and published by different people.

This cover was almost certainly hand-coloured over the original print. A number of printing establishments employed hand colourists before colour printing was perfected. This particular work is probably just pre-Victorican and has been included as an excellent example of an earlier style. The Regency look of this picture is more refined than the majority of its Victorian successors.

The shop shown on the cover opposite was the music publisher's own premises in Old Bond Street and the inscriptions in the window advertise other favourite music published by them and sung by Madame Vestris among others.

Music covers underwent an enormous change from Maxim Gauci to Alfred Concanen, not always for the better. However, with the developing technology of printing, there was more scope for the artist and the music covers show how these opportunities were taken.

Perhaps it was fortunate for Brandard, Concanen and their contemporaries, that they did not altogether outlive their usefulness. They worked productively until the end but without retaining the fame which they had originally commanded. They died more or less unrecorded. There were no obituaries or public manifestations of grief, that so many famous painters of their day received. But they have lived on in their work and it has been left to later generations to pick up the pieces.

Buy a Broom: *Maxim Gauci*

THE BAVARIAN GIRL'S SONG

The Words by

D.A.O'Meara.

Buy a Broom!

Sung (IN CHARACTER) by

MADAME VESTRIS,

With the most enthusiastic Applause.

Arranged expressly for her by

Alexander Lee.

Price 2

LONDON.

Mayhew & Co. Music Sellers to the Royal Family. No. 17 Old Bond Street.

Bibliography

BEAUMONT & SITWELL (1936) *Romantic Ballet in Lithographs of the time,* London, Faber & Faber.

BELLEW, Sir George, K.C.V.O. *St George's Chapel, Windsor,* London, Pitkin.

BOLITHO, H. (1949) *The Reign of Queen Victoria,* London, Collins.

BURCH, R. M. (1910) *Colour Printing and Colour Printers,* London, Sir Issac Pitman & Sons Ltd.

CHANCELLOR, E. B. (1925) *Pleasure Haunts of London,* London, Constable & Co.

CHAPPELL'S Music Magazine (1869)

COURTNEY LEWIS, C. T. (1928) *The Story of Picture Printing in England During the Nineteenth Century,* London, Sampson Low, Marston & Co. Ltd.

DINNAGE, P. (1962) *An Exhibition of Victorian Lithograph Song Covers,* London catalogue for an exhibition at the Museum St. Galleries.

DISHER, M. W. (1950) *Pleasures of London,* London, Robert Hale Ltd.

HYATT KING, A. (1950) *English Pictorial Music Title Pages* 1820-1885, reproduced by courtesy of the Trustees of the British Museum, from a paper read at a meeting of the Bibliographical Society.

IMESON, W. E. (1912) *Illustrated Music Titles,* London.

MACINNES, C. (1967) *Sweet Saturday Night,* London, Macgibbon & Kee.

MANDER, R. & J. MITCHINSON (1965) *British Music Hall,* London, Studio Vista.

NOVELLO & Co. Ltd. (1961) *A Century and a Half in Soho,* London, Novello & Co.

NOVELLO & Co. (1887) *A Short History of Cheap Music,* London, Novello, Ewer & Co.

SITWELL, S. (1948) *Morning Noon and Night in London,* London, Macmillan.

SCOTT, H. (1946) *The Early Doors,* London, Nicholson & Watson.

VIZETELLY, H. (1893) *Glances back through Seventy Years,* London, Kegan Paul, Trench, Trubes & Co. Ltd.

WATFORD, E. (1779-1885) *Old and New London,* London, Cassell & Co. Ltd.

The Business Directory of the Manufacturing and Commerical Cities of England (1864).

Acknowledgements

The authors would like to thank the following for their advice and assistance: the late Mr James Brydone, Mrs Alfred Concanen, Mr Derrick de Marney and Miss Eileen de Marney, Miss Cecilia Fellner, Mr and Mrs Kenneth Snowman, Mrs Phillis Warshaw, Mr John Foster White; the librarians and staff of the British Museum Library, St Bride's Institute Printing Library, the Victoria and Albert Museum and the Imperial War Museum.